For Our Beloved Mother

I Choose

A Life I Love Living

A Journey Towards Happiness
Through Self Awareness

Maurice Legendre

Levity Publishing

Asheville, North Carolina

Copyright © 2015 by Maurice Legendre

All rights reserved. No part of this book may be reproduced in form or by any means, electronic or mechanical, including photocopying, recording, or by any information storage or retrieval system, except for brief passages quoted for the purposes of review, without permission in writing from the publisher.

This book and its contents are not intended to diagnose, treat or cure anyone of physical or emotional illness. It is only an invitation to experiment; the benefits and responsibilities of such actions lie solely with the reader.

ISBN Number: 978-0-9893234-0-6

Cover Design by Maurice Legendre
Illustrations by Krystalyn Dawn Norton
and Maurice Legendre

Levity Publishing
Suite # 115
129 Bleachery Blvd.
Asheville, NC 28805

www.levitypublishing.com
Contact at
info@levitypublishing.com

Anything I
clearly imagine
greatly desire
enthusiastically work upon
and passionately appreciate
shall inevitably
become my reality.

Special thanks
to my loving mother
and supportive editor,

Joy Star Smith

who has
inspired me
all my life
to look inside
and know myself.

Table of Contents

Exploration of Self

Choice 2
Choosing self-awareness.

Notice 6
Observe thoughts, feelings,
actions, and expectations.

Pain 12
Connect with the emotional self
and allow pain to surface.

Explore 22
Explore the complexity of the
inner self with conscious intention.

Clearing 34
Accept past experiences to lessen
their influence on present choice.

Developing Intentional Interaction

Language 48
Speaking the changes in thoughts,
feelings and perspective.

Support 64
Creating the support to face
difficult changes and thrive.

Experiment 72
Proactively creating a new
energetic and social dynamic.

Self-Responsibility 82
Taking responsibility for
choices and their effects.

Choose 100
Choosing a life to love living.

Evolution 116

Introduction

This is a book about being human. It is about the thoughts and feelings that come up every moment. Whether they are conscious or unconscious, we live most of our lives greatly influenced by these surfacing sensations and stories. As you read this book you are invited to put yourself in the "I" position. Talk yourself through this process and reflect on your own experiences. As you read, thoughts will undoubtedly come up for you about your life, which is the purpose of this book. The more you can open to the thoughts and sensations that arise for you, the more you can know yourself and deepen the process of growth and discovery. You are encouraged to make these words your words and embrace their meaning in your own life. This is not an instruction book about how to live your life. It is an invitation to explore yourself in a new way; to learn to understand the inner workings of your own being, to bring peace into your heart through self-trust, and to share that grace with the world.

This is a book about choice. It is about the feelings and thoughts that shape your perception of the choices available. To change the way you experience life, you must choose to do so. Like selecting your food, clothing and hairstyle, you can also deliberately choose your attitude, focus and language. In this way you discover and re-create yourself by consciously choosing how to interact with your experiences. Rather than experiencing thoughts and emotions as reactions, you can use them to provide direction and stability. The more you guide your own human experience, the more feedback you get from life and the greater your range of awareness. Small and dedicated choices can start a landslide of self-discovery and unearth some of your deepest truths. When you walk this path, life will offer you many ways to know yourself. Each step will present itself as you choose to love the life you live.

Changing the Internal Dialogue

Words are not just a means to communicate with each other. Words are the medium through which we understand ourselves. The words we think and use can be the key to personal growth, or to perpetual suffering.

We humans learn to communicate in a particular language such as English from a very young age and as a result the patterns of our language become the basis for the structure of our thoughts. We naturally adopt and use familiar words and phrases for communication and in our minds. However, by doing so, we continually reaffirm established perspectives and opinions. So when we desire to change our living experience and seek relief from damaging habits, it is necessary to go all the way to the foundation of our thoughts, which are built from the words that we use everyday.

By changing our words we give ourselves mental authorization to pursue new avenues of thought. When we think about others and ourselves with different words, we can more comfortably hold new

I have presented this book to you in the first person format so that you can make these words your words. The intention is to help you develop new and empowering ways to speak and think. By adopting a new mental vocabulary, you are changing the thought structure through which you create your attitude and approach to life. In this way you explore more than just the concept of changing how you relate to yourself. You actually reshape your thoughts by changing the content of your spoken words and internal dialogue. The reading then becomes the practice and every time you speak, it is an exercise in becoming more conscious and self-aware. Life becomes your classroom to study your own nature and build the self-understanding that can bring you happiness.

Everything you need to know about yourself is there inside you waiting to be discovered.

All you need to do is choose.

My Experience of Finding Choice

Though I wrote this book based on my own experiences, I consider it to be much more about life and the experience of living than it is about me. I feel inspired to tell a little bit about my story to convey the experiences that pushed me to write this book and dive heart-first into the turbulent waters of human emotion. For me it has been a story of far off lands and unknown feelings. Fears that broke the weakest parts of my heart and forged a courageous compassion to keep breathing and living through my hurt. I traded the cold suffocating sadness of disappointment and despair, for the hot rage of confusion, pain and feelings of injustice. Yet by fully allowing myself to be engulfed by that emotional fire, I found a warm sense of peace, acceptance and grace that has taught me a new way to live.

The pursuit of understanding my thoughts and feelings has been a lifelong endeavor. In my late teens and early twenties the intensity of my emotions grew to be a daily flood of feelings that I neither understood nor felt that I could control. Amid confusion and despair,

I wrapped my heart in an acceptance of disappointment that protected me from vulnerability and heartbreak. I hid my sadness, stayed busy, worked on being happy and yet guarded myself around intimate connections that could hurt me. I accepted this as my life, even though on the inside I still felt a deep longing.

After college I continued to live with a growing sense of restlessness. My fears of commitment and stagnation accompanied by my longing for options, adventure and the unfamiliar motivated me to travel to the Hawaiian Islands. After a fiery social month on the Big Island, I went to Kauai and found myself suddenly alone in a strange and beautiful land. Questions, doubts and fears flooded into my mind and heart. I felt lonely and disappointed, angry with myself for having chosen to come here.

Triggered by a lifetime of disappointments and self-criticism, I felt disoriented and dismayed by the ocean of emotions washing over me. Determined not to run away from what I was feeling, I found a secluded beach, built a sand pyramid and camped out on my own for three days.

In those three days something changed in me. I realized that I had become so familiar with my own sadness and disappointment that I had begun to wear it like an emotional raincoat that I never took off. For fear of getting wet/hurt I shielded myself. Yet I forgot to take it off when it wasn't raining and feel the warmth of the sun and of love. So, sitting there in the sunshine on a beautiful Hawaiian beach, I decided to learn how to take that raincoat off and open to the joy and love of the sun's warmth. I sat and felt, and thought, and wrote. How could I remove the shield that had protected me from fear yet kept out joy as well? For years I had skirted between love and fear, afraid to surrender to either. Yet there on that beach a concept grew in my mind. It is all a matter of choice; all change starts with a choice. Over those three days the inspiration to explore choice grew and expanded in my heart. On the third night a storm pushed the waves higher up the beach and in the dark washed my pyramid back into the sand. I awoke the next morning, still alone and yet no longer lonely. I carried that vision with me as I traveled on and really began to see how I create my own emotional as well as physical reality.

I returned from Hawaii feeling confident and inspired. Yet when I got home, I crashed. So many of the fears I thought I had put behind me came back in a rush. I was facing my deep disappointments and feelings of lack in a whole new way. With my emotional raincoat partially removed, I felt much more vulnerable to despair as I started opening up to joy and love. Indundated by new and intensified emotions, I sought shelter in the inspiration that I had received on the sunny beach in Hawaii. In the next few months I wrote about what I was feeling and the concepts that helped me understand them. Those writings I condensed into short passages that are here in this book. In a few months I had a first draft as a small pocket book.

As I read my book over and over again I realized that the wisdom that came from the pages was not reflected in my own heart. Though I conceptually understood the words I had written, I had not yet had a chance to live the choices I was realizing existed. I began to doubt myself and to question the truth of what I had written. I printed my first copy and bound it by hand, to read and edit and strive to live by.

I left home shortly thereafter and over the next few years, I traveled around the world with my girlfriend and my little hand-bound pocket book. In those years I learned how to dream big, to live through my disappointments and to find the other side. I learned how to support myself and ask for what I needed, as well as how to stretch to support the needs of another. While traveling in countries I never knew existed, I discovered things about myself that felt equally as foreign. I found compassion for the suffering of others, and realized that I could hold the same compassion for my own suffering. I learned from the Cambodians that no pain from the past can prevent us from striving for a loving future. India showed me that even the poorest people have an inner wealth that could light up my heart with the generosity of their radiant smiles. In Australia I realized that "no worries mate" is a mantra as much as a catch phrase. And some young men in Morocco reminded me that we are all evolving our cultures as well as our selves forward into a future that has no boundaries except the ones we impose upon ourselves. We live in changing times and we are all finding our own path as best we can. We can never have too much courage when we strive for a loving future and a peaceful heart.

At times I still feel fear and sadness, yet I can also feel the warm light of love unhindered by perpetual disappointment. Through the twists and turns of my winding path, I learned that I can be hurt and still thrive, that I can love and not hold back. I have come to accept myself and trust myself to create peace in my own heart. I can laugh at my flaws and be grateful for what I enjoy about myself. More than anything, I have learned that I can choose to love the life I live; by infusing my life with gratitude and love, living itself becomes more and more meaningful.

I am still a student of this book and have evolved as it has. Though I continue in my process of self-discovery, I now offer this book to you, so that you may learn to dream big and courageously find yourself. As the following passages have helped me open to love, face my fears and live a life I love living, I sincerely wish the same for you.

-Maurice Legendre

Exploration of Self

Choice

While no one can tell me who I am
or what will make me happy
I can always choose to take steps
to self-discovery and
pursue my own satisfaction.

From confusion and pain I am motivated
to find deeper personal truth.

From a desire to have peace
and love in my life
I am inspired to actively seek
its source within myself.

I choose to open up to myself
and explore who I am.

To be happy in my life
I need to be comfortable within myself,
and this requires looking within
and being honest about what I discover.

Paying attention to my thoughts,
emotions, inspirations, and inner-voices,
helps me guide and deepen
my own experience.

By connecting within,
I learn about and can change
how I relate to myself
and to the world.

I take each step
focused on positive growth,
willing to face, accept
and let go of old patterns.

I stop lying to myself about what I feel
and hiding from old painful memories.
I choose to go deeper to explore
my needs and inner complexity.

Discovering my inner truth
allows me to identify and clear
reactionary forms of thinking
and attitudes imposed by others.

Building a deep connection within
to my emotions and needs
gives me the opportunity to act
from intentional self-fulfilling choices.

I start changing the way I talk about
my experiences and myself by using words
that support my desires and say what I mean.

By adopting new ways to support myself
and create nurturing interactions with other people,
I move through the fear that I am unable
to create what I need in my life.

I empower myself by taking responsibility
for my attitude and choices.
I embrace the power of choice
to face fear, grow stronger, choose joy,
and create peace in my heart.

When I live in awareness
and acceptance of my own nature,
I can love, support and be at peace
with the being that I am.

I can truthfully and lovingly be myself
in every moment of my life.

Notice

When I look inside, I notice that:

I am often frustrated

by things or people in my life.

I feel limited in my choices

and controlled by my emotions.

My disappointments seem to

define my daily life experience.

Even on the good days

I find something

to complain about.

Growth and change come
when the acceptance of sadness and fear
brings a calm pursuit of joy:

How can I be at peace
with myself?

How can I be more accepting,
grateful and enthusiastic
about what is in my life?

How can I stop resisting fear
and have love as my companion?

How do I find the happiness
that is within me?

In order to change my life
I need to know who I am.

When I choose to deepen
my knowledge of myself,
I notice that a lot of
suffering and confusion
comes from not knowing
what my feelings and needs are.

By choosing to identify what
my core needs are,
I'm discovering what is necessary
for me to experience happiness.

I choose to examine

the habitual methods

I currently use to get what I need.

I learn how I am effective

and ineffective

at creating happiness

for myself and others.

Through awareness of what I need

and how I choose to get it,

I can change the way

that I engage with the world

to consciously and effectively

create the experiences I desire.

I notice that I feel a lot of things

and that I have a lot of intense reactions,

yet I don't always know why

or where they come from.

I notice that I feel helpless

in these moments.

I feel like there is a stranger

inside me.

I notice a need

to get connected

with my inner self,

so that I may understand

and be at peace with who I am.

In order to feel satisfied

and able to attract

the feelings I desire,

I need to know how I feel right now.

To know how I feel,

I need to be willing to look within.

To see clearly within,

I need to accept all that I find.

To accept myself,

I need to be completely open with myself.

When I choose full self-awareness,

from an attitude of

self-love and patience,

I can know satisfaction.

Pain

I breathe,

I Notice,

Ouch!!!

Why am I in pain?

Trying to avoid fear and pain

I made myself numb.

Feeling is the first step

towards reconnection with myself.

Breathing deep,
I choose to stay present
with my emotions.

Facing inner emotional pain
is like dealing
with a dirty room,
it gets easier
every time I go in
and clean up
a little bit more.

The most painful moments

in personal growth

are after

I have become aware,

and before

I break out

of old negative patterns.

Breathing deeply.

I choose to focus

on finding excitement

and opportunity,

rather than clinging

to resistance,

during my challenging

experiences.

Being present

with my emotional

growing pains

is an essential part

of my expanding

self-awareness.

I choose to let go

of resentment

for having

to face my life's

difficult moments.

I accept

that pain

is a natural

sensation.

I soothe my pain

like I would

attend to a hurt child,

with love

and kindness.

I accept

that suffering is a choice

to take pain personally

and believe that pain

is punishment.

My pain does not

require me to suffer.

I let go of

suffering

with deep

compassion.

I go to the

depth of my sadness

and allow myself to

cry and clear out

the pain.

The floodgates open

and my tears

wash away

my sorrow.

After fully letting go

I feel empty.

I enjoy feeling empty,

drained of my

tears and tension.

I choose

to allow the

space within

to fill with quiet love.

With my mind at ease, I notice

the sensations in my body.

Do I need . . .

. . .food?

. . .sleep?

. . .intimacy?

. . .privacy?

. . .to cry more?

I listen when my body

tells me what it needs

to feel at ease,

balanced and loved.

I choose to
give my body
what it needs
to be nurtured,
with care
and gratitude.

Explore

With calm body
and open mind,

I explore
how I interact
with new thoughts
and emotions.

How do I create

my own joy and suffering?

Am I open to new

feelings and situations,

becoming excited by them

and experiencing joy?

Am I closed to new

sensations and circumstances,

feeling deep resistance and suffering?

Fear can become excitement

by connecting to life energy

through deep breathing,

unconditional love or

complete acceptance of the moment.

Is my first reaction to
shut down?

Do I let my fear push
away what I desire?

By letting my fearful thoughts
separate me from
creativity and courage,
I build walls around my goals.
In this state, finding
a positive solution seems
very difficult and out of reach.

I choose to make fear my
guide rather than my jailer.

Is my first reaction to

open up?

Does my fear motivate me

to create positive options?

By facing fear with

innovation and courage,

I am able to keep an open heart

and mind in all my experiences.

In this state I feel a deep connection

to my dreams, empowered

to make them a reality.

I choose to find a way to expand

and learn in every situation.

I open my mind

to who I am

and who I am becoming.

It is the expressing

of my essence

that brings a deepened

sense of self.

I hold love for myself

and welcome the

gifts I have to offer.

Every morning

I say hello

to my reflection.

I take a little time

to explore how

I'm feeling today.

I process my fears

by verbally

expressing them.

While looking into a mirror,

I speak honestly to myself,
just letting out whatever comes
to mind, no matter how silly.

I acknowledge any fears I have
and talk to myself
about fun ways to address my concerns.

While listening to my reflection,
I pay attention
to what kind of voice is talking
and the emotional charge
in the tone of my words.

Am I talking from . . .

my wounded needy child self?

my authoritative parent self?

my loving centered self?

or

another part of myself?

How do I respond to my

different voices?

My child voice asks questions

and expresses its needs and fears,

while my adult voice guides,

offering words of comfort

and experience.

Through fun
and sad times,

I learn
how to love myself
as the hero
and as the fool,

and
find happiness
in who I am.

When I choose

to dedicate myself

to living in love,

fear

will only help me

grow stronger.

I let

my dreams

draw me

to open,

grow,

explore,

and love.

I discover
each moment
with a
caring, positive
and
empowered
attitude.

Clearing

As I integrate new

knowledge and experiences,

I let go

of what is no longer

beneficial for my growth.

I choose

to face my old

painful memories

with a passion to

grow and be healed.

When choosing to change,

I am not finding fault

or punishing myself

for past actions or beliefs.

I honor the choices I made as valid

and important for me at that time,

and I choose to make

different decisions

based on what I value

right now.

Each moment is a

stepping stone to the future,

not a ball and chain to the past.

When I feel a build-up of
anxiety, sadness, resentment,
or other intense emotions
that I'm ready to clear out,

I find a supportive friend
or my own reflection in a mirror.

I take five minutes to complain
about how I'm feeling.

Breaking the tension
of suppressed emotions
through verbal expression,
I let go of collected negativity
by talking about it.

After my five minutes
of clearing, it's time to think
about what I can change.

I take some time
to talk about at least one thing
I can do differently
to change the situation
starting right now.

I choose to move beyond
the hurt feelings
from my past.

When I feel trapped

in angry feelings

I explore ways to reconnect

to my heart:

I take a moment

and focus on my body.

I feel my anger like hot, toxic liquid,

trapped and building up pressure

within my skin.

I breathe deep

into my physical discomfort.

I imagine blowing up a bubble

of light and calmness

within the core of my being.

I visualize this light
bubble pushing up through
my fear and anger, like air,
easily rising through the water
of my emotional body.

This light bubble breaks through
the limits of my anger
and I breathe a renewed
connection to life.

I hold this space open
and focus on my breath.
I allow loving energy to fill me,
while my anger evaporates
and drains away.

I acknowledge
any disappointment,
resentment or blame
I carry from the past.
Instead,
I hold gratitude for
what my experiences
have given me.

I choose to
let go of defensiveness
in order to clear attachment
to old painful experiences.

In this way the pain can be
accepted, moved through
and left behind.

I choose
to take off the
burden of guilt
and shame.

I experience them
like a giant backpack
filled with the
weight of the world.

I drop this burden
from my shoulders
and stand up tall,
light and
free to be me.

To be more alive

in the present moment,

connected

to my current feelings,

I clear attachments

that keep me trapped

in past emotions

and stuck

in established reactions.

To let go of old experiences

is not to push away the past,

it is to hold the past

with acceptance.

I choose
to envision
a healthy
and nurturing
transformation
as I identify
and move away
from old patterns.

To change, I embrace
the mystery of
new possibilities.

Like a warm,
gentle massage
that soothes away
tension,

I attend
with love
to the needs
that my fears
illuminate.

I am grateful

for the opportunity

to look inside

and

grow stronger.

*Developing
Intentional
Interaction*

Language

As I strengthen

my awareness

of my feelings,

I notice

their connection

to my thoughts.

When I consciously

choose to alter

my way of thinking,

I also shift

my language.

As I consciously

select the words

that say what I mean,

daily communication

becomes

a constant opportunity

to reexamine

the thoughts and feelings

that shape

my attitude and approach

to life.

I can't.

It's impossible.

I won't.

When I use self-defeating language,

it inhibits my conscious

and subconscious mind.

Restrictive words prevent

my natural ability to explore an issue,

conceive of a positive solution,

or deepen my understanding.

I can.

It's possible.

I will.

When I use
self-encouraging language
it helps me further the learning
process. Positive and supportive
words encourage and actualize
my abilities, allowing me to
work at and accomplish
anything I desire.

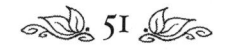

I'm always late.

I can never do anything right.

I always feel this way.

When using absolutes I am simply
lying to myself, for there are no absolutes
in an ever-changing world. It is just another form of
restrictive language that separates me from my
goals, and the current moment,
while undermining my potential growth.

I choose to change my statements
when I catch myself using absolutes.

I'm a little late this time.

Sometimes I make mistakes.

Right now this is how I feel.

When I talk in situational terms,
I acknowledge my current experience
with honesty and without judgment.
Using situational language engages me
in the present moment as it is,
while leaving the future open to change.

I choose to talk about each specific moment
from my own perspective.

Do I use the word **But**

when talking about my desires?

When using **But,**

I create separation in my options.

"I'd love to go play **But**

I have to work today, so I can't."

"I want to change, **But** I need to be courageous."

Or

I can use **And** when I talk about the different

things I want, **And**

remain open to all possibilities.

"I'd love to go play **And**

I've chosen to work today,

so I'll make time for both."

"I want to change,

And I need to be courageous."

I choose to banish

the negating and self-limiting word

"But"

from my language.

Using it creates conflict

in my stated desires,

and excludes multiple options.

Instead,

I choose to use words

that support my desire

for a variety of things.

Using **"And"**

allows me to experience all my needs

as genuine possibilities

in my life.

Occasionally
my tone of voice
is more charged
than I intended.

I notice there are
emotions in my words
that I was unaware
I was experiencing.

I choose to examine
these feelings
so I can more fully
understand myself.

Being aware of

my feelings

and attending

to my own needs

allows

me to

communicate

in a

supportive

and loving way.

I notice my tendency to react

and take little comments

or actions of others as an

intentional personal insult.

I choose to let go

of immediate, under informed,

defensive reactions.

Instead.

I notice that we each speak

and act from our own

deep emotional needs.

Often unconscious of these needs,

they shape our perceptions and

greatly effect our interactions.

I choose not to take
the unintended or hurtful
actions of others personally.

I accept that those actions
are motivated by their own
unmet personal needs.

I choose to hold peaceful,
loving energy in my being
through all my interactions.

I

choose

to focus

on the needs

within the words

and actions

of others.

I choose to focus

on the desires

that motivate

my own words.

I choose

to consciously change

the words that I use

to more accurately represent

my own needs and intentions.

Through awareness of my words

and my tone of voice

I gauge where I am making progress

and where I still have undiscovered

issues waiting to be addressed.

I find new ways

to use my language

to gain understanding

and connection

with myself and others.

I choose

to use my words

in a gentle,

informative manner

to attract pleasure

and satisfaction.

I choose

to speak

with love.

Support

I Need Support!!!

I need to support myself first

to truly appreciate

what others have to offer.

Realizing the value of

taking care of my own needs,

I choose to do so with

love and patience.

What are a few ways that

I can support myself?

I am aware that there are some things
I like about myself, and other things
I wish were different.
I am okay with not currently
being all that I desire to be.

In order to support and encourage
myself to learn and change,
I must support and accept myself
as I am right now.

If I cannot love myself as I am now,
I will not be able to love myself
as I will be.

I choose to lovingly accept myself
through all my disapointments.

I sit quietly, look into a mirror,

or simply stop what I'm doing

and focus on being in the present moment.

I pay attention to my breath

and notice what is happening in my body.

I envision an abundance of peaceful silence waiting

below the surface of my being.

I spread this peacefulness over my body

like a healing ointment,

rubbing it in with loving intention.

I build a fountain of peace in

my heart, just feeling happy,

supported and loved.

I find a safe place, a symbol,

a piece of music,

a sound, or a color

that helps me feel at ease.

I choose a word or image

that connects me

with this peaceful feeling.

I use my word or image

to calm me

when I feel off balance

and need support.

I support myself

by consciously giving myself

the loving energy I desire.

In order to receive the support I desire,
I need to ask for the support I require.

I cannot assume that others
will automatically know
what I need to feel
supported and loved.

I take responsibility
to ask for what I need.

By asking for what I need,
I am helping myself understand
what is really important to me,
while helping others
to support me.

I choose

to support myself

by speaking clearly

and acting directly

to get my needs met.

I choose to be
the support
I want to have
in the world.

I choose to open

a connection

to my inner self,

and let the love

that supports me

flow freely

from inside.

I choose to live
in an environment
that supports me.

I choose to engage

in situations

that nurture me,

so that my love

can be easily shared

among open hearts

and grow

to its greatest potential.

Experiment

I experiment

with different ways to act

in old familiar situations

in order to unlock myself

from the habits of the past

and live in the full potential

of the present.

When I don't know

what will bring

me happiness,

I make a guess,

try it out,

and guess again.

Sometimes I learn

about who I am

by trying to be

who I'm not.

The only way I can change

is to try something new.

I accept that discomfort

can come with experimentation,

and it is only a sensation

along the way.

I break the limitations

of fear with courage.

I let go of certainty

in order to discover

my potential

over and over again,

until the mystery

of uncertainty

becomes

a joy in my life.

I learn about myself

through experiments

and experience.

I study

my unique

complexity with

childlike wonder,

loving the exhilaration

of daily self-discovery.

I choose to focus

on the wonderful ways

that I personally

experience joy.

I play with using

notes, charts, journals,

games, activities,

images, words

or phrases

that help me stay

consciously mindful

along my path towards happiness.

I choose to focus on my state of being,

clarifying my intentions daily

so that the universe

can help me experience

what I desire.

I make a list

of physical activities

to use when I feel stuck in

emotions like fear, grief,

anger or frustration.

I breathe deeply,

ecstatically dance,

move,

laugh,

cry,

sing,

run,

ride a bike,

make silly noises,

whatever works for me.

I use these
physical activities
to clear tense
and confusing energy
as well as create joy
and calmness inside my body.

While in these
peaceful moments,
I explore and identify
the root causes of my emotions
and attend to each one directly.

Looking deep within,
I am honest
and gentle with myself
about what I find.

I am my own

science experiment.

I choose

to have fun

while learning

to be joyful.

Self-Responsibility

I choose to be
fully response-able
when nourishing
my body, mind
and spirit.

I am
responsible
for my mood
and actions.

When I am satisfied,
I am grateful,
relieved and pleased.

I choose to resist

acting impulsively

from an attitude

of frustration

and anger,

thus fostering

more violent energy

in the world.

I choose to take

my unhappy feelings

as a sign

that it's time

to get motivated

and do something proactive

to satisfy my needs

and fulfill my dreams.

Everything in my life

comes from the choices

that brought me here and now.

Some choices were loving,

some hateful,

some brought pain,

others joy.

I let go

of shame, anger, guilt,

or other attachments

to the past.

I honor them all

as choices that made me

who I am today.

Everything in my life
comes with a choice,
a choice
to like it or not,
and a choice
to do something about it.

I don't blame anyone,
anything or myself
for my
current situation.

I learn from the
choices I have made
as I follow
my own path
through life.

Every mistake
I have ever made
has taught me
how to make
wiser choices now.

I accept
disappointments
as reminders to
clarify my desires
and continue learning.

I choose

to be present

and focused

in the moment.

I choose

to make

compassionate

intentional

choices.

I choose

to pay attention

to the

repeating situations

in my life;

I accept

that they are patterns

I recreate.

I notice that I have some
ingrained unpleasant dynamics
with my loved ones.

When the interaction is painful
I often hastily blame others
for these feelings.

Taking several deep breaths,
I acknowledge my part
in the situation.

Focusing on what I can do
to create what I need,
I let go of resentment and blame.

I let go of the need for
praise or blame to
define my life experience.

I choose not to base my
decisions on the
expectations or opinions
of others.

I encourage other people
to be true to themselves
making their own choices,
while I choose
simply to be me.

When my feelings get hurt,
I take time to examine
what unfulfilled need
is causing this pain.

I breathe some love into the pain
and forgive the people involved,
for they are a means
to discovering myself.

I choose to learn about myself:
I discover my needs and limits,
and act to communicate them
before I get hurt.

When I am

sad or excited,

fearful or ecstatic,

angry or compassionate,

it creates a vibration

that affects everyone,

especially

those closest to me.

I choose to take
responsibility
for transforming
my own fear, anger
and sadness.

I contribute
to creating a
peaceful human race
by becoming a
peaceful human being.

I step into
awareness
and accept
my fears.

I realize the
boundlessness
of my abilities
when acting
from a place
of love.

I strive

to understand

the things in life

that I choose not to

agree with,

so that I don't

feel the need

fight against

the things in life

that I do not

understand.

As my inner light brightens,
my gratitude for life
fills my heart.

My sense of self-love
gives me acceptance,
appreciation, patience
and responsibility
for the being
that I am.

I don't have

to be

perfect,

to be

perfectly

true to myself.

Choose

I choose,

because

it is the single

greatest power

that I possess

in this life.

I choose
to enjoy, honor
and take care of
this amazing planet
and treat every
living being
with kindness.

I choose to change

my opinion,

perspective

and lifestyle

as I discover

and integrate

new information

and experiences

into my emerging

and transforming

sense of self.

I choose to act
with gentle honesty,
offering openly
what I have to share
and asking directly
for what I need.

I choose to bring
balance and harmony
into my life
with caring words.

I

choose

to open,

learn, grow,

let go, adapt,

connect, explore

and love,

every day

of my life.

I
choose
to find
limitless joy
in my own life,
letting pain
show me
where even
more joy
is possible.

I choose to foster

the loving,

present,

responsible,

compassionate,

passionate,

delighted

adult

that is uniquely

me.

I choose to encourage

the fun,

playful,

emotional,

inquisitive,

adventurous,

inspirational,

open-hearted

child within

me.

I choose

to treat myself

with kindness.

I choose to do

one thing today

that brings more beauty

into the world

around me.

I choose

to be a loving being,

creating a loving home

on Mother Earth.

I choose

to be awake,

aware and engaged

in every moment

of my life.

I am open

because I choose

to grow from

my experiences.

I am grateful

because I choose

to be here now,
alive and
in love with life.

Happiness is my sail
on the sea of life.

Joy is the light
that guides me.

Passion is the wind
that moves me.

Love is the life force
that fills me.

And my choices
are as numerous
as the ripples of the sea,
stretching from
horizon to horizon.

As
I Choose
to Be...

I Am.

Evolution

If you're coming to the end of this book and don't feel any different than when you started, that's fine. Life is not a race. We each grow in our own ways, at our own pace and according to our own desires. As you build a deeper friendship with yourself, set aside any ideas of competition. Don't let anyone else get in the way of you knowing who you are. Be patient and persistent, even when you don't feel immediate changes. Often I have found that I wake up one morning and reflect on the past few months and suddenly realize so much has changed and I didn't even notice it happening. Be prepared to be surprised. There are probably things about yourself you just don't know yet. What a wonderful adventure it can be to discover those parts of yourself. Remember always to breathe. Breathe into the joy and let it flow through your body. Breathe deep into the pain, feel it, and breathe it out again. Nothing within you is off limits to you. Give yourself full access to explore the inner workings of your being and be gentle with what you find. You are a unique and miraculous living being; nurture yourself and watch yourself grow.

41473177R00078

Made in the USA
Charleston, SC
02 May 2015